My Big Book of MAZES

Amazing MAZES

Table of Contents

To parents: AMAZING MAZES

In this section, your child will complete activities designed for mastering pencil control, which is a precursor to writing. Your child will trace lines through fun mazes to help develop his or her pencil control and spatial reasoning ability. By playing with these amazing mazes and drawing lines any way he or she wants, your child will practice the pencil skills necessary to write letters and numbers later on. Such practice will also help your child acquire the ability to concentrate, which is a crucial study skill.

Additionally, as children go through a maze, they usually follow this pattern: they see the whole maze, as well as parts of the maze; they interpret and understand the way they will reach the exit; and then, they actually trace the line. In this way, mazes help develop children's ability to interpret what they see and move their pencils according to that understanding. In addition, they have to reason and interpret how to reach the exit over and over. Through this trial-and-error method of finding the right answer, children are able to develop the abilities to reason, interpret, and understand.

The activities in this section will help your child develop his or her fine motor skills. If your child is interested in developing similar skills, please refer to the appropriate book from our other Basic Skills products for further work.

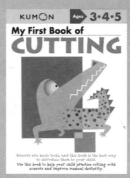
My First Book of
CUTTING

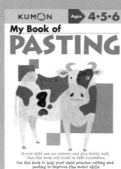
My Book of
PASTING

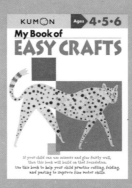
My Book of
EASY CRAFTS

How to hold a pencil properly

There are several ways to teach children to hold a pencil properly.
Here is one example.

1 Help your child form an "L" shape with his or her thumb and forefinger as pictured here. Place the pencil against the top of the bent middle finger and on the thumb joint.

2 Now, have your child squeeze the pencil with the thumb and forefinger.

3 Check the way that your child is holding the pencil against the picture to decide whether or not it is the proper way.

It can be difficult for a child who does not yet have enough strength in his or her hand and fingers to hold the pencil properly. Please teach this skill gradually, so that your child will remain interested and willing to hold a pencil naturally.

To parents Have your child trace the path with his or her finger, then with a pencil. For extra practice, have your child continue to trace the path with different colored pencils. Give your child plenty of encouragement and praise.

Draw a line from the arrow (→) to the star (★) by following the path.

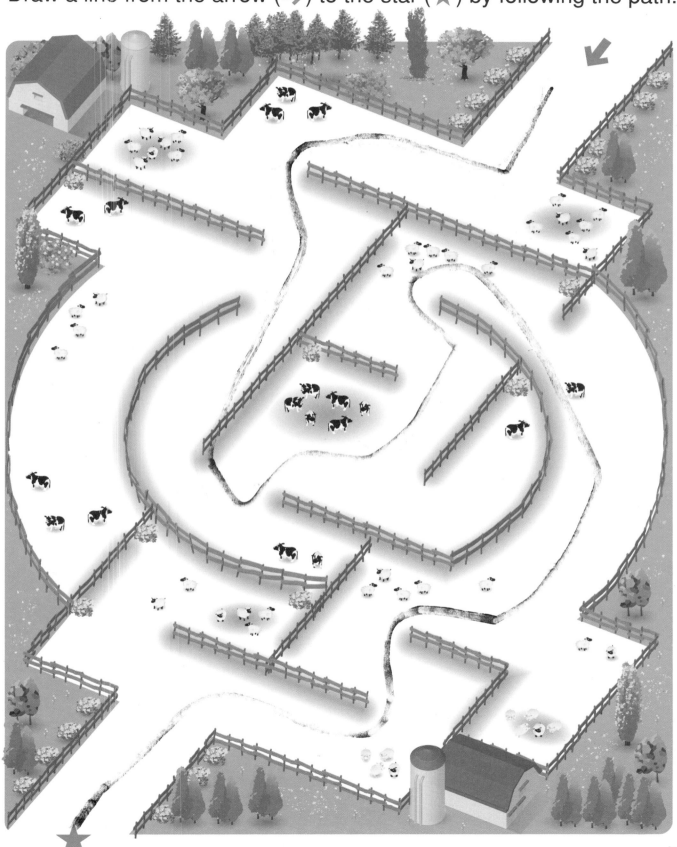

3

Draw a line from the arrow (→) to the star (★) by following the path.

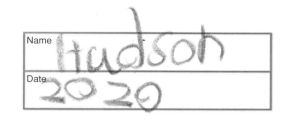

Name Hudson
Date 2020

Draw a line from the arrow (➡) to the star (★) by following the path.

Draw a line from the arrow (→) to the star (★) by following the path.

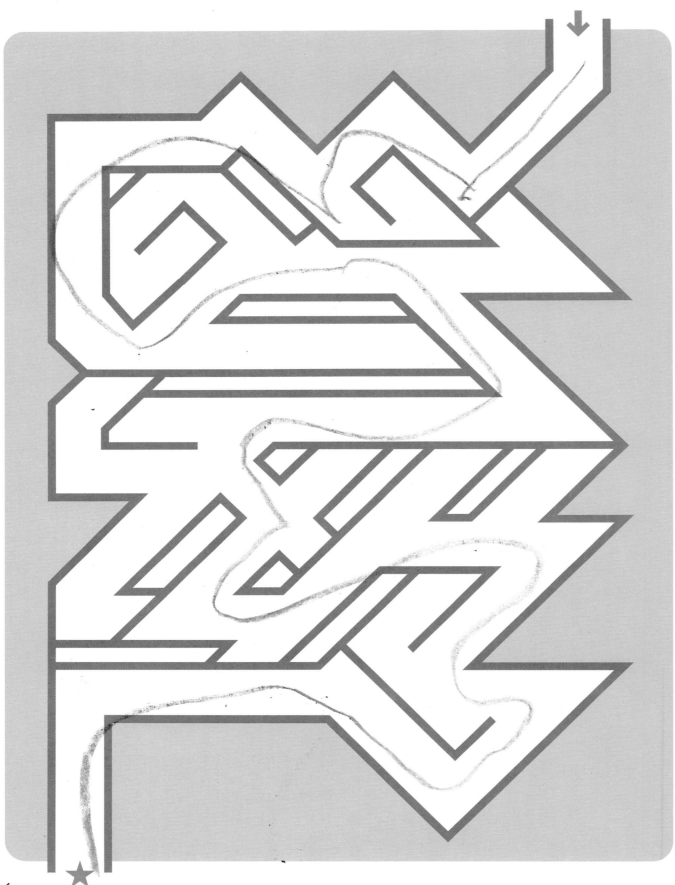

Name Hudson

Date 2020

Draw a line from the arrow (→) to the star (★) by following the path.

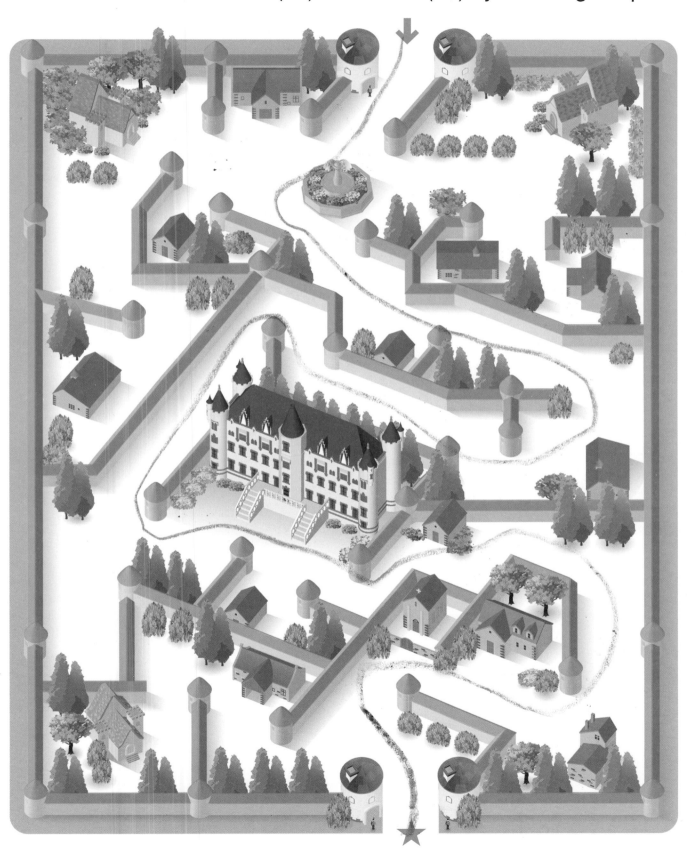

Draw a line from the arrow (→) to the star (★) by following the path.

Name: madson
Date: 2020

Draw a line from the arrow (➡) to the star (★) by following the path.

Draw a line from the arrow (→) to the star (★) by following the path.

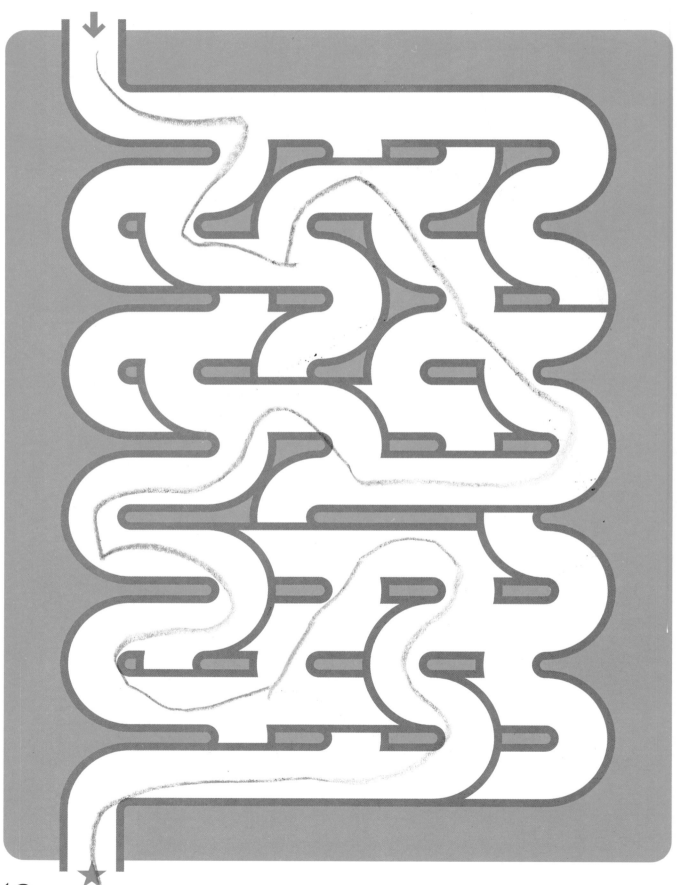

Name Hudson
Date 2020

Draw a line from the arrow (➡) to the star (★) by following the path.

Draw a line from the arrow (➡) to the star (★) by following the path.

6 Super Speedway

Draw a line from the arrow (→) to the star (★) by following the path.

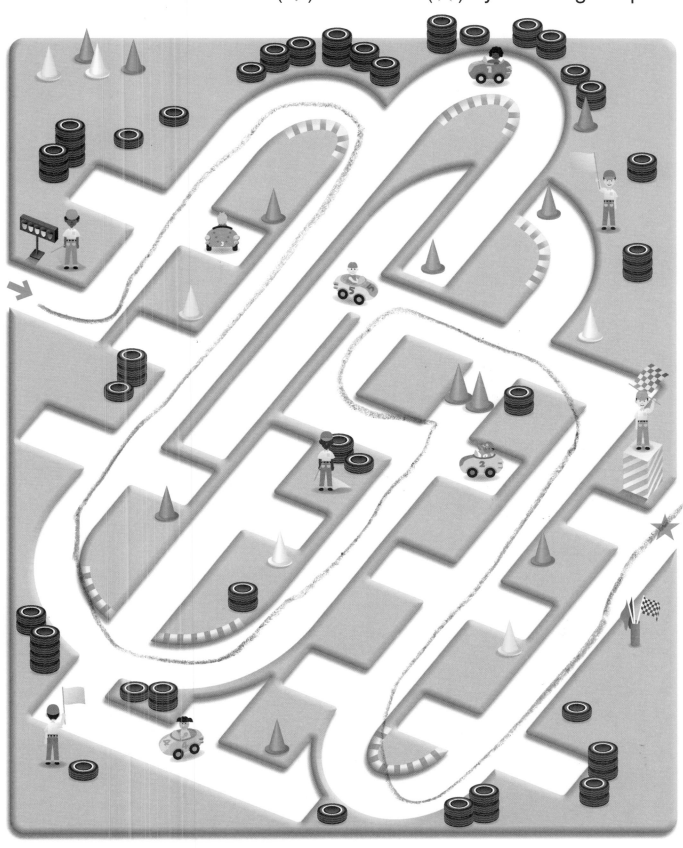

13

Draw a line from the arrow (➡) to the star (★) by following the path.

Name Hudson

Date 2020

Draw a line from the arrow (➡) to the star (★) by following the path.

Draw a line from the arrow (→) to the star (★) by following the path.

Name Cooper
Date 2020

Draw a line from the arrow (➡) to the star (★) by following the path.

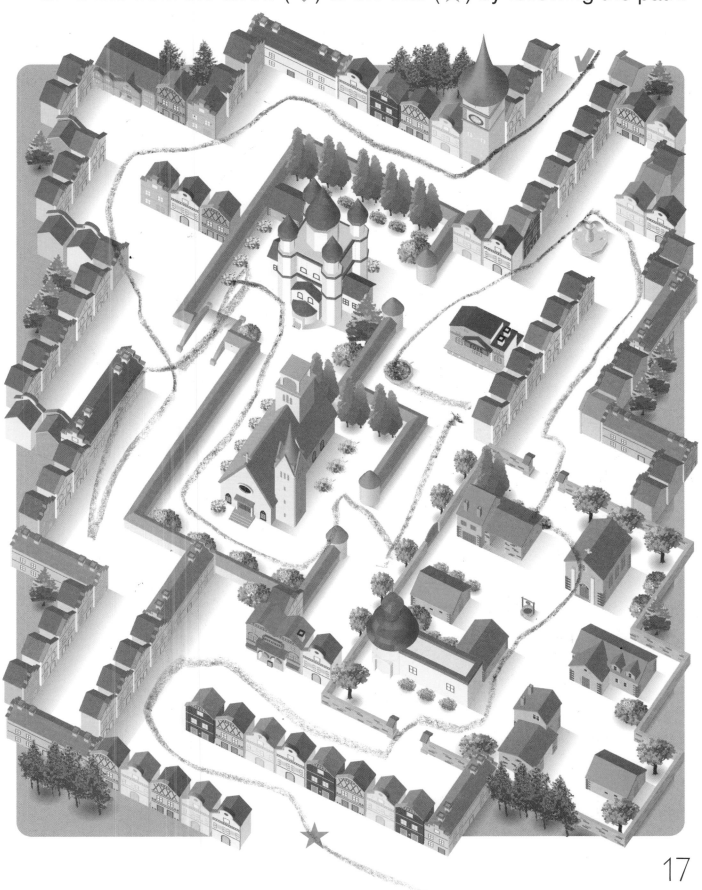

Draw a line from the arrow (→) to the star (★) by following the path.

Name Cooper

Date 2·5·20

Draw a line from the arrow (→) to the star (★) by following the path.

Draw a line from the arrow (→) to the star (★) by following the path.

Name

Date

Draw a line from the arrow (➡) to the star (★) by following the path.

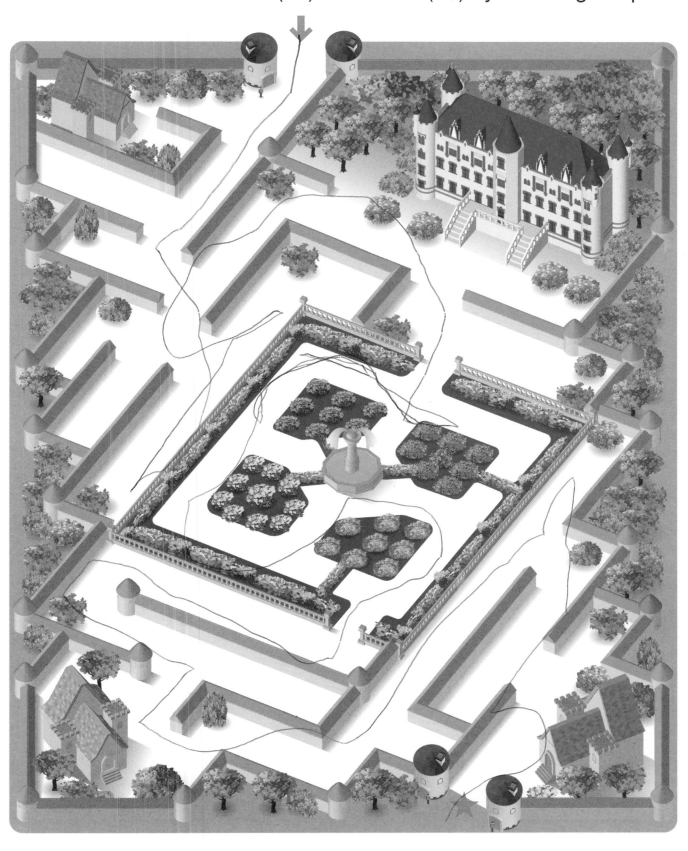

Draw a line from the arrow (→) to the star (★) by following the path.

22

Where is my House?

Name Hudson
Date 2020

Draw a line from the arrow (→) to the star (★) by following the path.

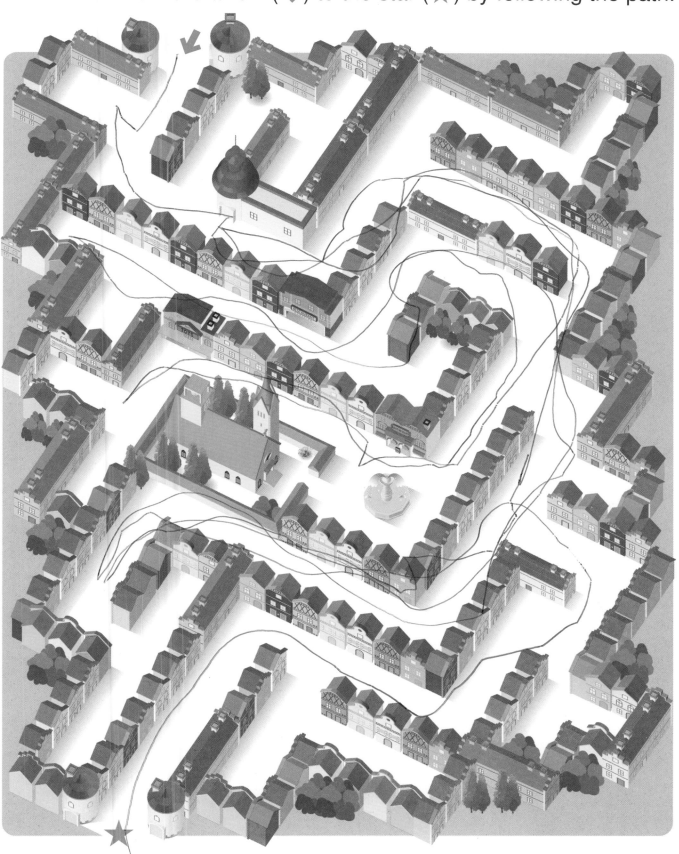

Draw a line from the arrow (➡) to the star (★) by following the path.

Name COOPer

Date 2021

Draw a line from the arrow (→) to the star (★) by following the path.

Draw a line from the arrow (→) to the star (★) by following the path.

On the Farm

Name Hudson
Date 2022

Draw a line from the arrow (→) to the star (★) by following the path.

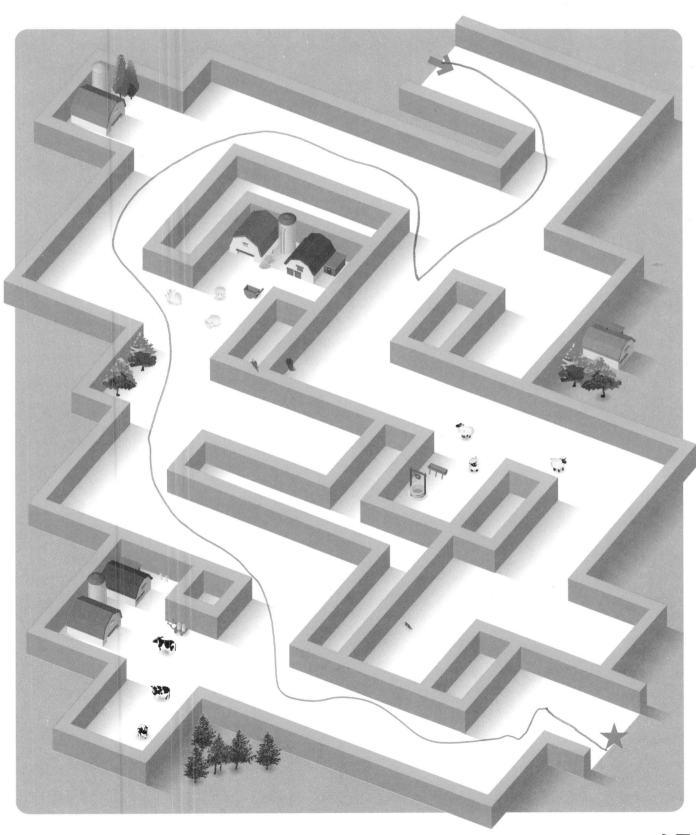

Draw a line from the arrow (→) to the star (★) by following the path.

Next Door Neighbors

Name Hudson
Date 2018

Draw a line from the arrow (→) to the star (★) by following the path.

Draw a line from the arrow (→) to the star (★) by following the path.

Name Hudson

Date 2022 sep 28

Draw a line from the arrow (➡) to the star (★) by following the path

Draw a line from the arrow (→) to the star (★) by following the path.

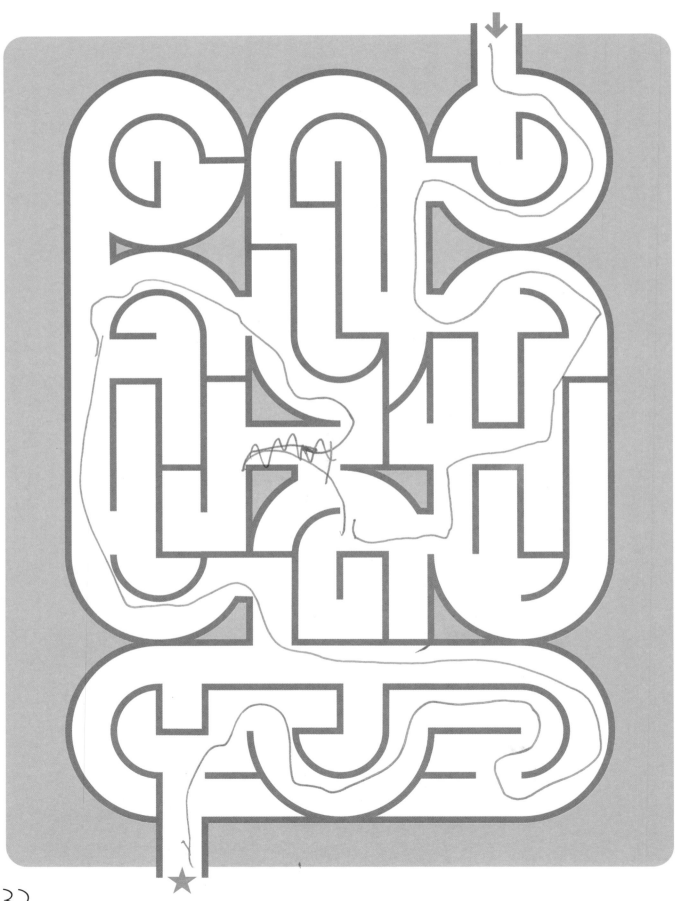

Through the Woods

Name
Hudson
Date
2022 sep 26

Draw a line from the arrow (→) to the star (★) by following the path.

Draw a line from the arrow (→) to the star (★) by following the path.

17 Fish Bubbles and Crab Claws

Name Hudson
Date 2022 sep 26

Draw a line from the arrow (→) to the star (★) by following the path.

Draw a line from the arrow (→) to the star (★) by following the path.

36

Name: Hudson
Date: 2022 Sep 26

Draw a line from the arrow (→) to the star (★) by following the path.

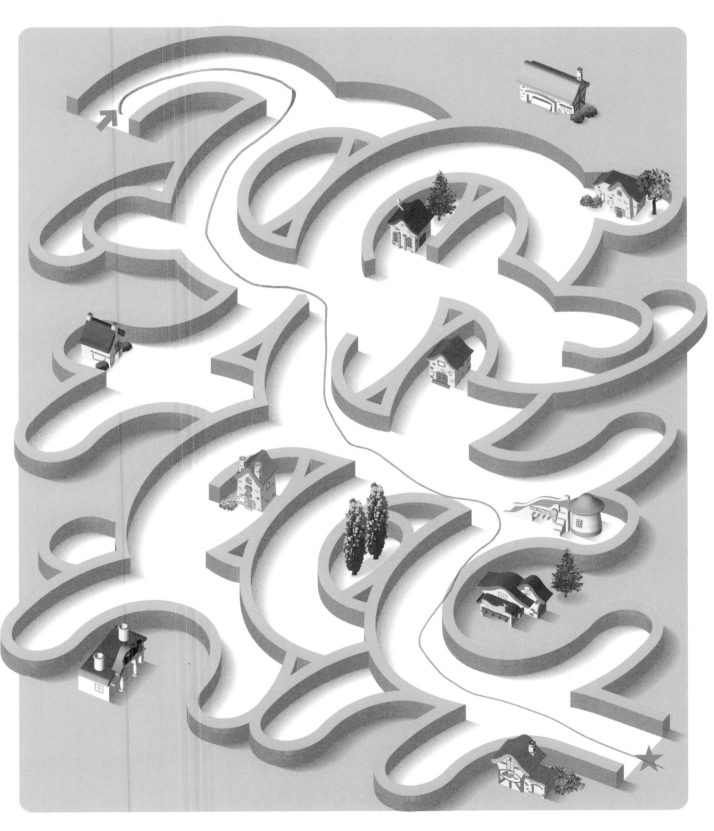

37

Draw a line from the arrow (→) to the star (★) by following the path.

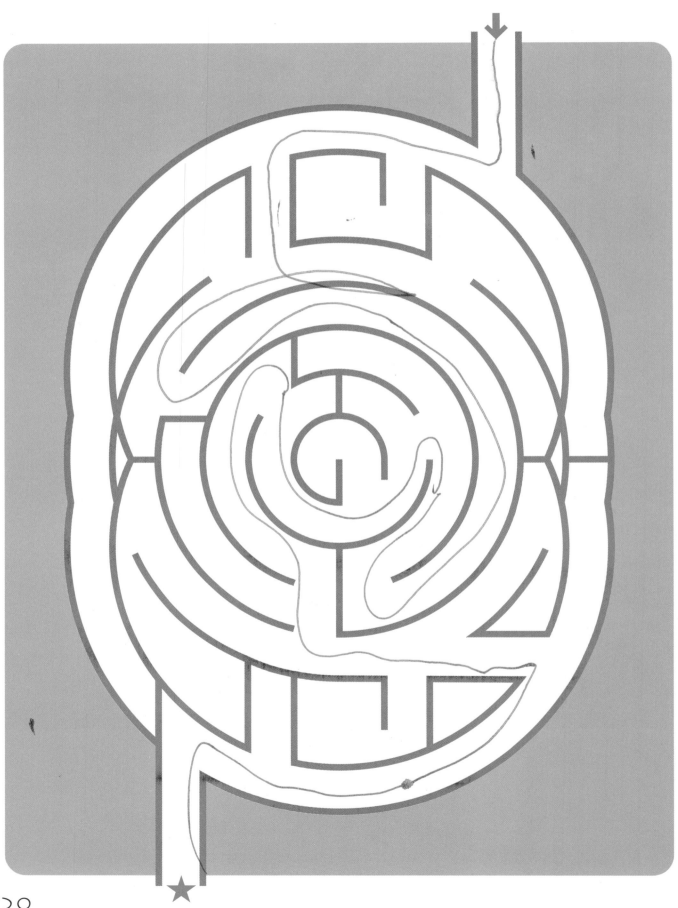

19 Zoom Zoom 500

Name Hudson
Date 2022 SEP 26

Draw a line from the arrow (→) to the star (★) by following the path.

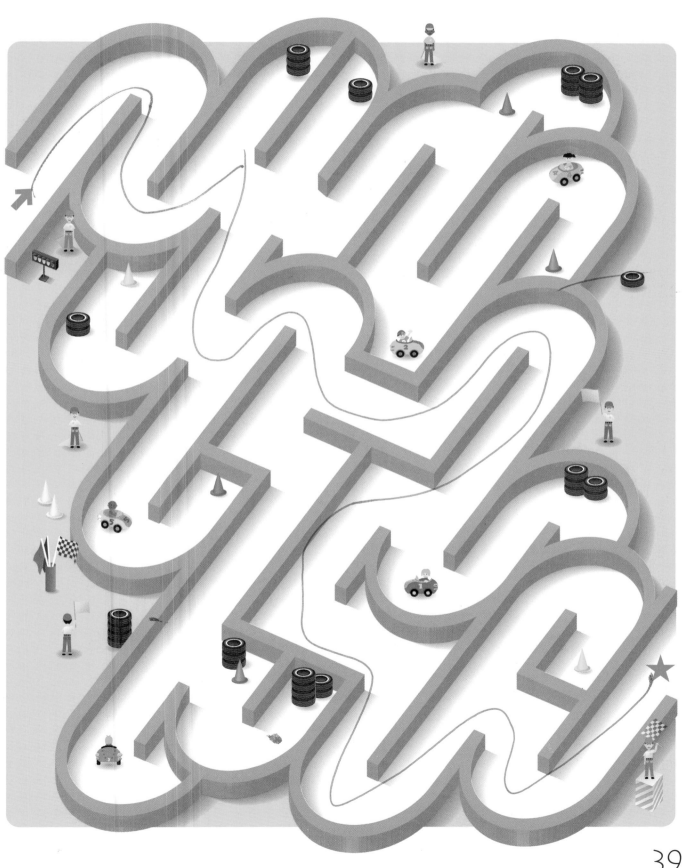

Draw a line from the arrow (→) to the star (★) by following the path.

40

Autumn Lanes

Draw a line from the arrow (→) to the star (★) by following the path.

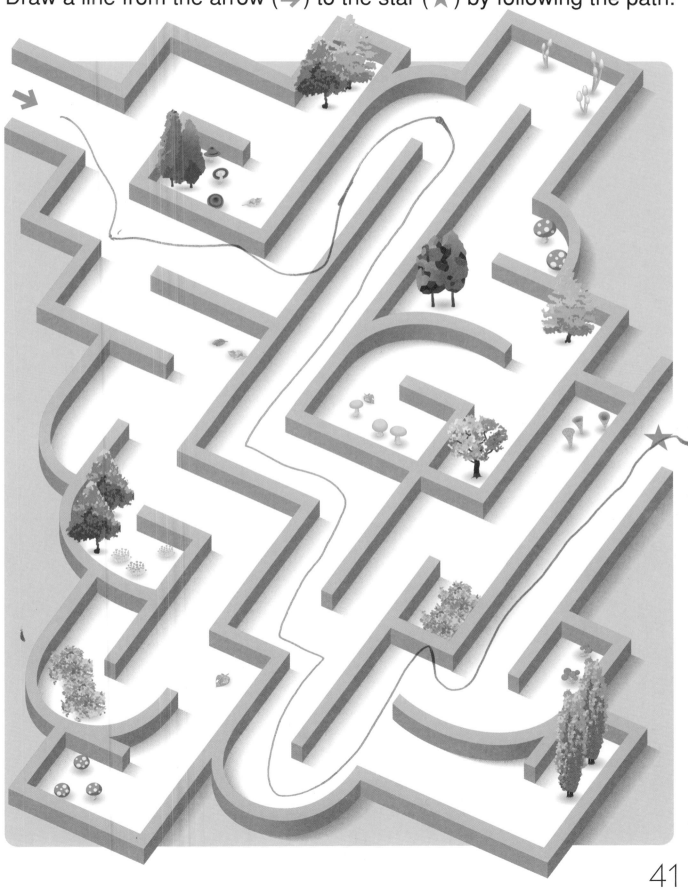

Draw a line from the arrow (→) to the star (★) by following the path.

21 Palace Walk

Name
Hudson
Date
2022.926

Draw a line from the arrow (➡) to the star (★) by following the path.

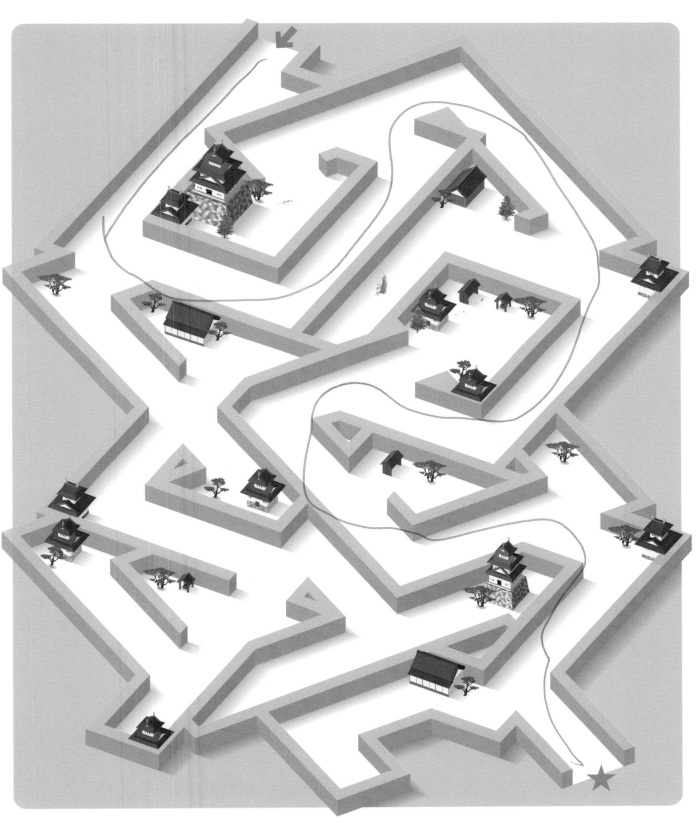

Draw a line from the arrow (→) to the star (★) by following the path.

Name Hudson
Date 2022 SEP 26

Draw a line from the arrow (➡) to the star (⭐) by following the path.

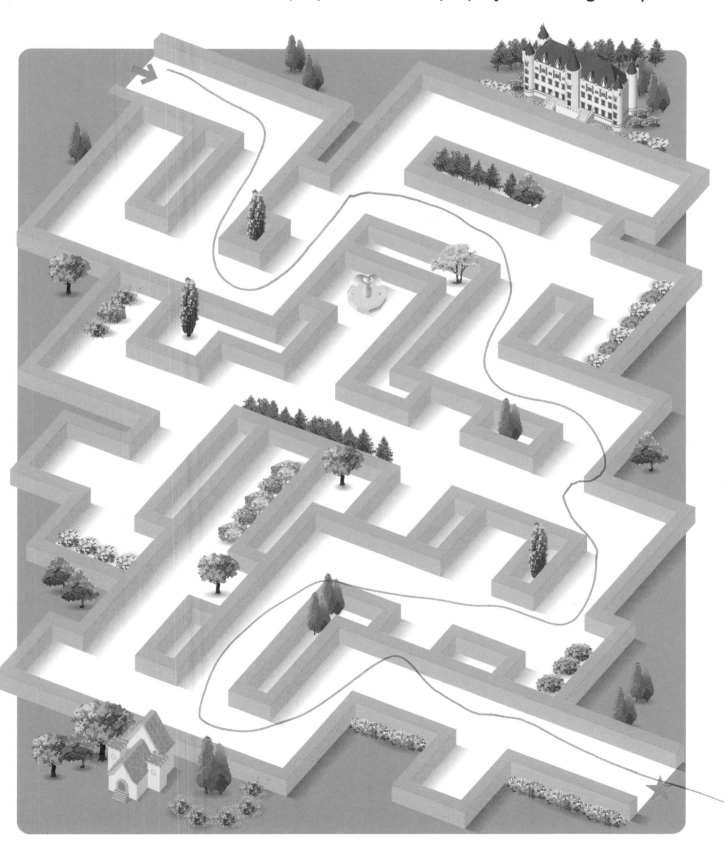

45

Draw a line from the arrow (➡) to the star (★) by following the path.

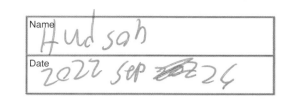

Name Hudson

Date 2022 sep 2022 26

Draw a line from the arrow (→) to the star (★) by following the path.

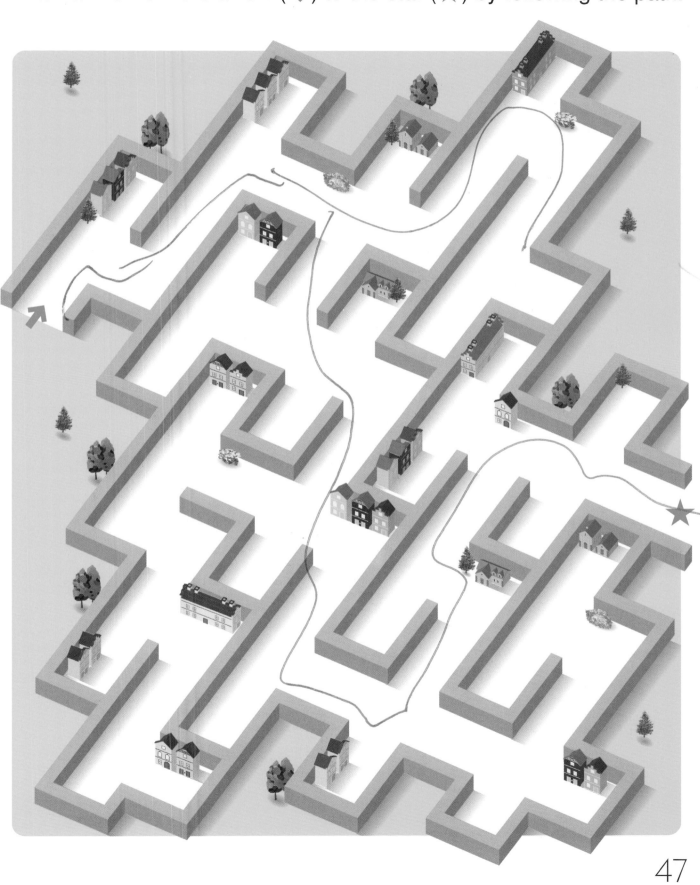

Draw a line from the arrow (➡) to the star (★) by following the path.

Prince's Pathways

Name Hudson
Date 2022 SEP 26

Draw a line from the arrow (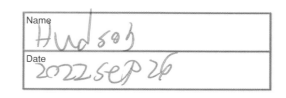) to the star (★) by following the path.

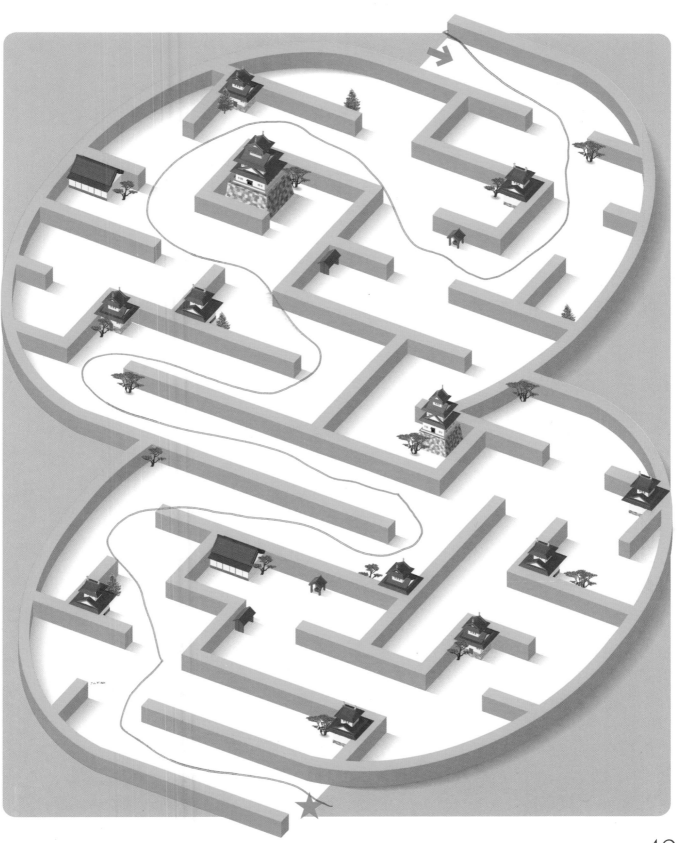

Draw a line from the arrow (➜) to the star (★) by following the path.

Name Hudson

Date Sep 26

Draw a line from the arrow (➡) to the star (★) by following the path.

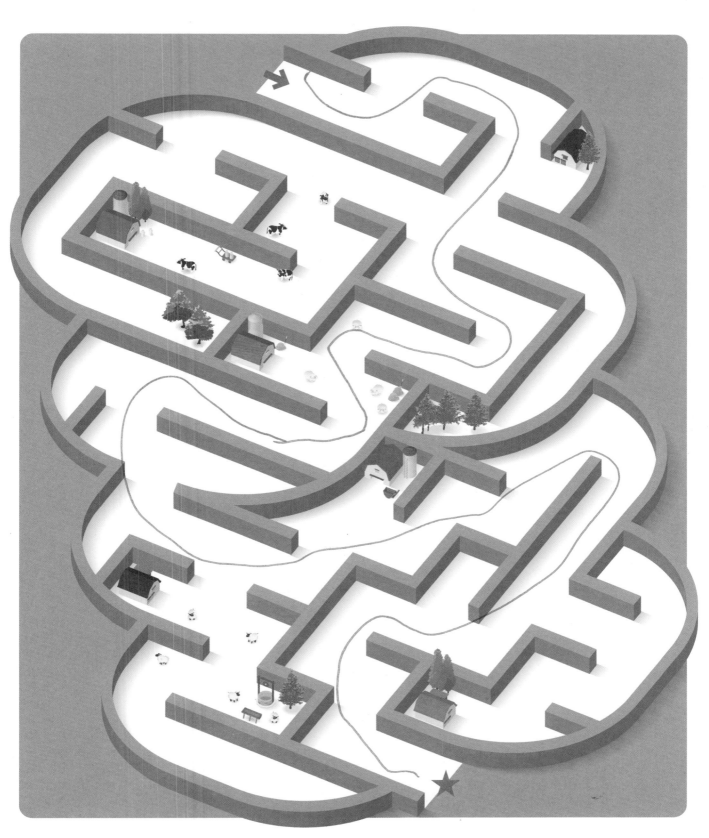

Draw a line from the arrow (→) to the star (★) by following the path.

52

Name 4udsan

Date 2022sep26

Draw a line from the arrow (→) to the star (★) by following the path.

Draw a line from the arrow (→) to the star (★) by following the path.

54

Gathering Garden Vegetables

Name
2022

Date
26 Sep 2022

Draw a line from the arrow (→) to the star (★) by following the path.

Draw a line from the arrow (→) to the star (★) by following the path.

Name: Hudson

Date: 2022 sep 26

Draw a line from the arrow (➡) to the star (★) by following the path.

57

Draw a line from the arrow (→) to the star (★) by following the path.

Cook

To parents
Starting with this page, the maze patterns are different from others in this section. Mazes on even-numbered pages have narrower paths and are more challenging. When your child completes each exercise, praise him or her.

Name: Hudson
Date: 2022 Sep 26

Draw a line from the arrow (→) to the star (★) by following the path.

Draw a line from the arrow (→) to the star (★) by following the path.

30 **Nurse**

Draw a line from the arrow (→) to the star (★) by following the path.

Draw a line from the arrow (→) to the star (★) by following the path.

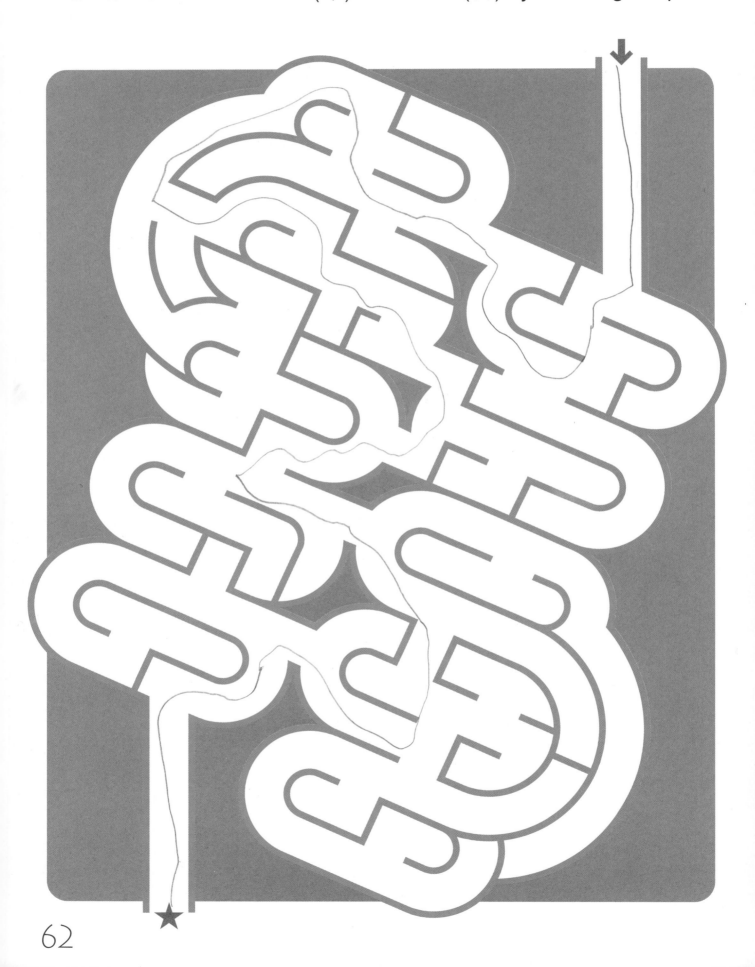

Draw a line from the arrow (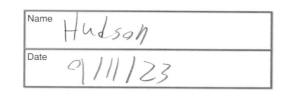) to the star (★) by following the path.

Draw a line from the arrow (→) to the star (★) by following the path.

Firefighter

Name Hudson

Date 9/11/23

Draw a line from the arrow (→) to the star (★) by following the path.

Draw a line from the arrow (→) to the star (★) by following the path.

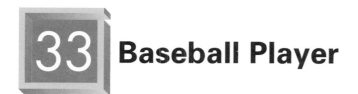

Baseball Player

Name: Hudson
Date: 9/11/23

Draw a line from the arrow (➡) to the star (★) by following the path.

67

Draw a line from the arrow (→) to the star (★) by following the path.

Ninja

Name Hudson

Date 9/11/23

Draw a line from the arrow (→) to the star (★) by following the path.

Draw a line from the arrow (→) to the star (★) by following the path.

Football Player

Name Hudson
Date 9/11/23

Draw a line from the arrow (➜) to the star (★) by following the path.

Draw a line from the arrow (→) to the star (★) by following the path.

36 Doctor

Draw a line from the arrow (➡) to the star (★) by following the path.

Draw a line from the arrow (→) to the star (★) by following the path.

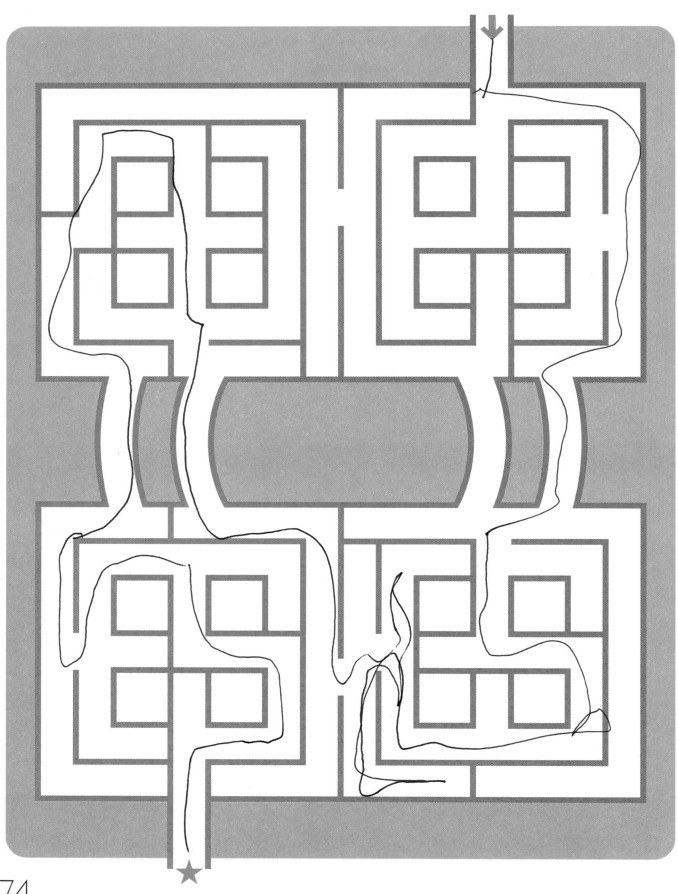

Name Hudson
Date 9/11/23

Draw a line from the arrow (→) to the star (★) by following the path.

Draw a line from the arrow (➡) to the star (★) by following the path.

Samurai

Name

Date

Draw a line from the arrow () to the star (★) by following the path.

Draw a line from the arrow (→) to the star (★) by following the path.

Draw a line from the arrow (➡) to the star (★) by following the path.

Challenge! ①

To parents
The maze on this page is different from the previous pages. Trace the practice path below with your child if he or she has difficulty. Make sure that he or she only draws vertical and horizontal lines, and not diagonal lines.

Draw a line from the arrow (→) to the star (★),
connecting only rabbit (🐰) to lion (🦁) or lion (🦁) to rabbit (🐰).

40 Farmer

Draw a line from the arrow (➡) to the star (★) by following the path.

Challenge! ②

To parents
The maze on this page is different from the other pages. Trace the practice path below with your child if he or she has difficulty. Make sure that he or she only draws vertical and horizontal lines, and not diagonal lines.

Draw a line from the arrow (→) to the star (★), connecting only bear ( ) to rabbit ( ) or rabbit ( ) to bear ( ).

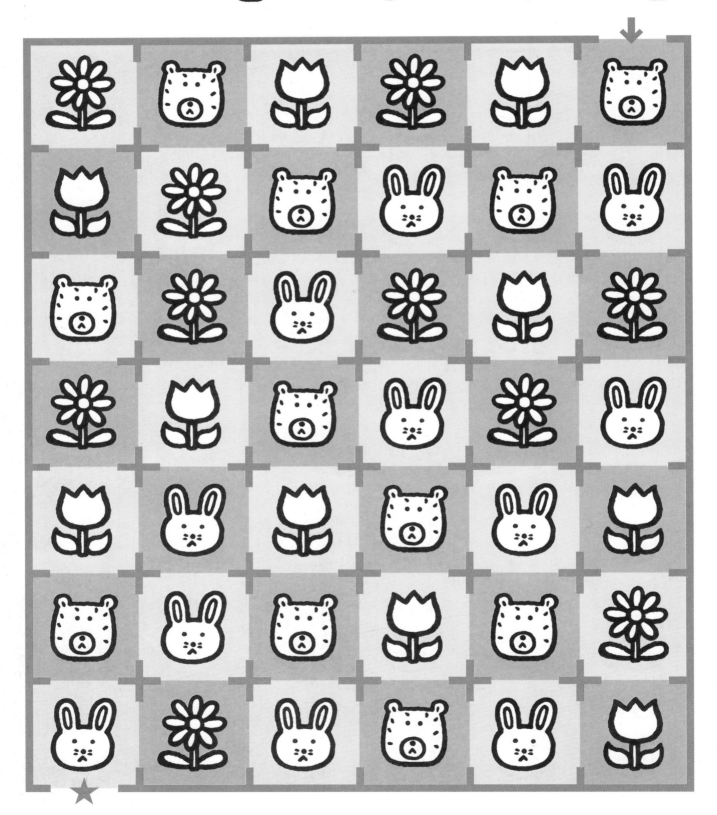

82

My Big Book of MAZES

MAZES: ANIMALS

Table of Contents

In this section, your child will complete animal themed mazes designed to help him or her master pencil skills, which are a precursor to writing letters and numbers. These basic mazes allow your child to develop spatial reasoning ability and practice the pencil control skills necessary for future learning.

First, your child will trace lines through simple animal mazes following clear directional indicators. Gradually, your child will complete more difficult mazes as his or her abilities improve. Mazes are a fun way for children to learn how to properly hold and use a pencil. Additionally, the trial-and-error method of solving mazes will develop your child's reasoning ability. Soon, your child will be able to properly gauge the correct path through each maze.

The activities in this section will help your child develop pencil control, which is essential for early writing skills. If your child is interested in developing other skills, please refer to the appropriate book from our Math Skills and Verbal Skills products for further work.

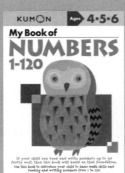
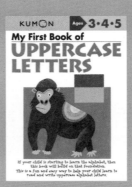
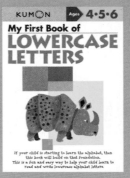

My Book of
NUMBERS 1-30

My Book of
NUMBERS 1-120

My First Book of
UPPERCASE LETTERS

My First Book of
LOWERCASE LETTERS

How to hold a pencil properly

There are several ways to teach children to hold a pencil properly.
Here is one example.

1 Help your child form an "L" shape with his or her thumb and forefinger as pictured here. Place the pencil against the top of the bent middle finger and on the thumb joint.

2 Now, have your child squeeze the pencil with the thumb and forefinger.

3 Check the way that your child is holding the pencil against the picture to decide whether or not it is the proper way.

It can be difficult for a child who does not yet have enough strength in his or her hand and fingers to hold the pencil properly.
Please teach this skill gradually, so that your child will remailn interested and willing to hold a pencil naturally.

1 Rabbit in the Carrot Patch

Name

Date

To parents
Have your child trace a path through the maze with his or her finger before using a pencil. Next, have your child use a pencil to complete the maze. When your child is done, give him or her plenty of praise.

Draw a line from the arrow (➡) to the star (★) by following the path.

Draw a line from the arrow (→) to the star (★) by following the path.

2 | Mouse in the Watermelon Patch

Name

Date

Draw a line from the arrow () to the star (★) by following the path.

Draw a line from the arrow (→) to the star (★) by following the path.

Beaver in the Corn Field

Name

Date

Draw a line from the arrow (➡) to the star (★) by following the path.

Draw a line from the arrow (➡) to the star (★) by following the path.

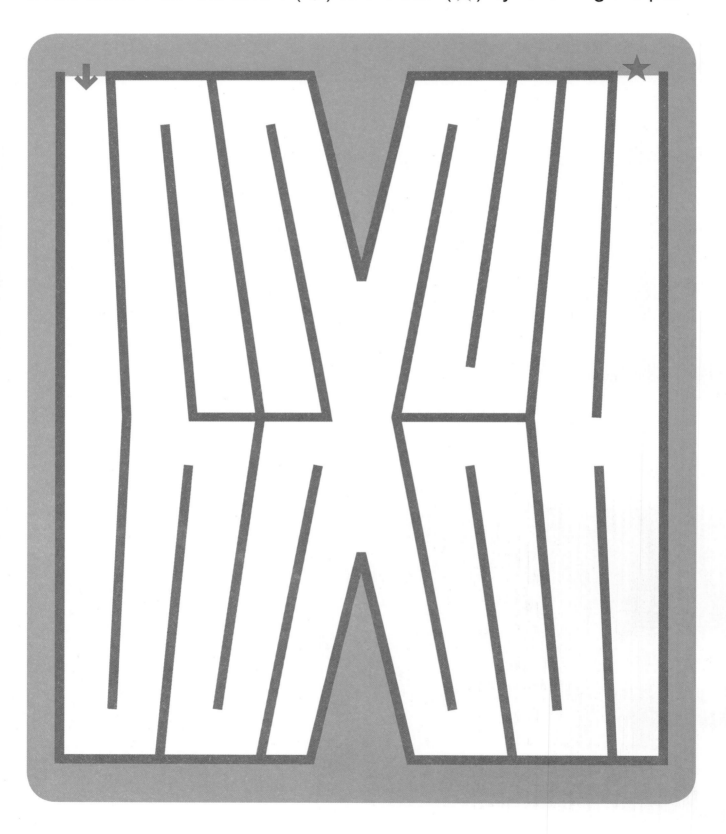

4 | Showering Cat

Draw a line from the arrow (→) to the star (★) by following the path.

Draw a line from the arrow (➡) to the star (★) by following the path.

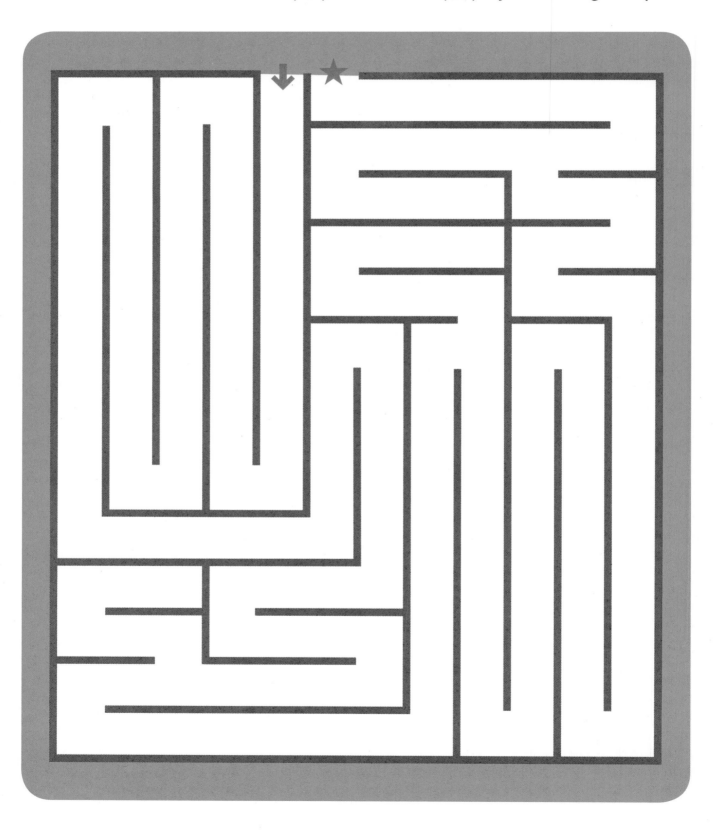

Name

Date

Draw a line from the arrow (→) to the star (★) by following the path.

Draw a line from the arrow (→) to the star (★) by following the path.

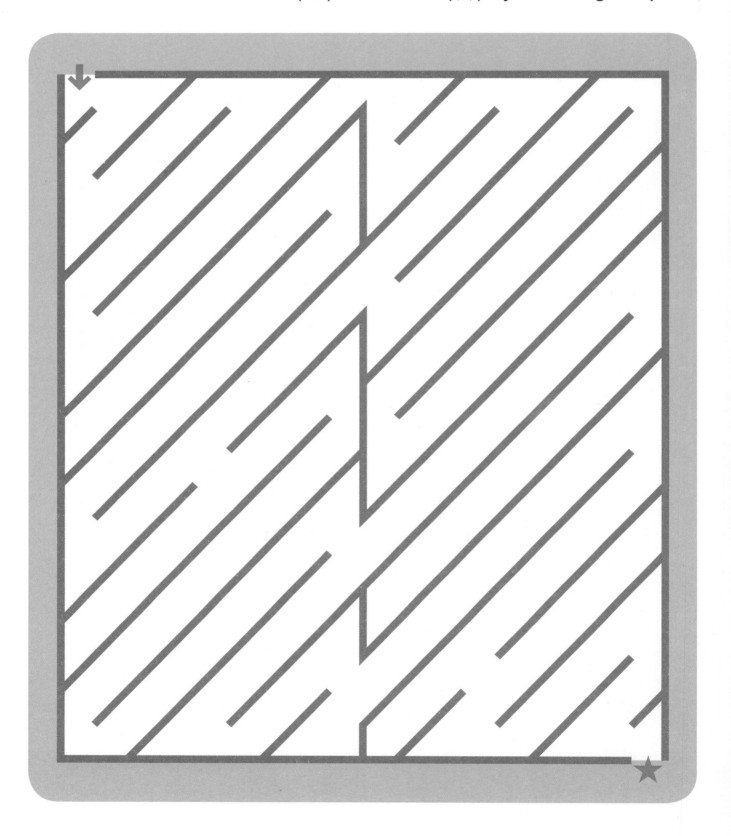

6 Singing Frog

Name

Date

Draw a line from the arrow (➡) to the star (★) by following the path.

Draw a line from the arrow (→) to the star (★) by following the path.

7 Bulldog in the Yard

Name

Date

Draw a line from the arrow (→) to the star (★) by following the path.

Draw a line from the arrow (→) to the star (★) by following the path.

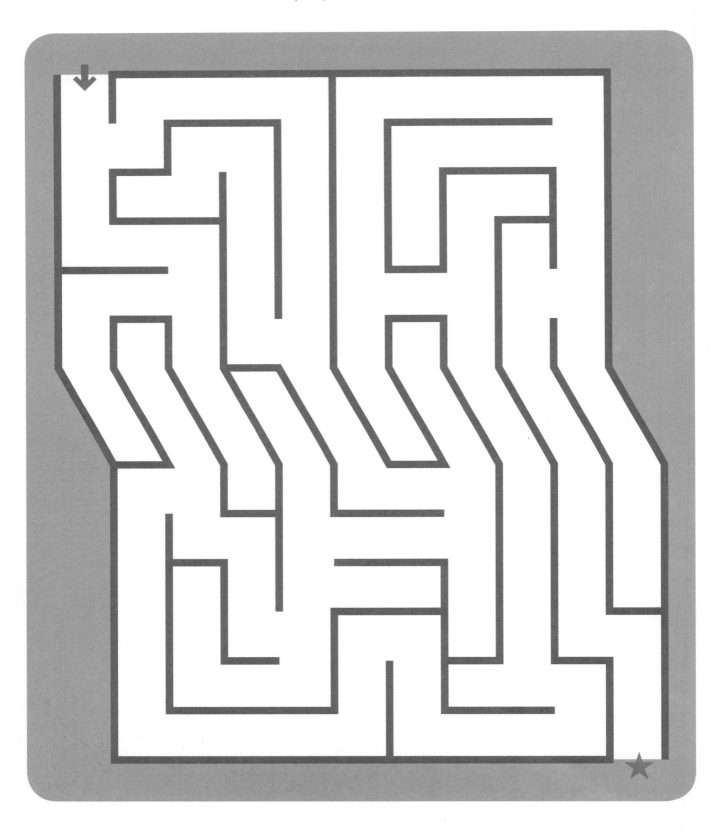

8 | Rhino playing Golf

Name

Date

Draw a line from the arrow (➡) to the star (⭐) by following the path.

Draw a line from the arrow (→) to the star (★) by following the path.

Soccer Squirrel

Draw a line from the arrow () to the star (★) by following the path.

Draw a line from the arrow (→) to the star (★) by following the path.

Rabbit on the Balance Beam

Name

Date

Draw a line from the arrow (→) to the star (★) by following the path.

Draw a line from the arrow (→) to the star (★) by following the path.

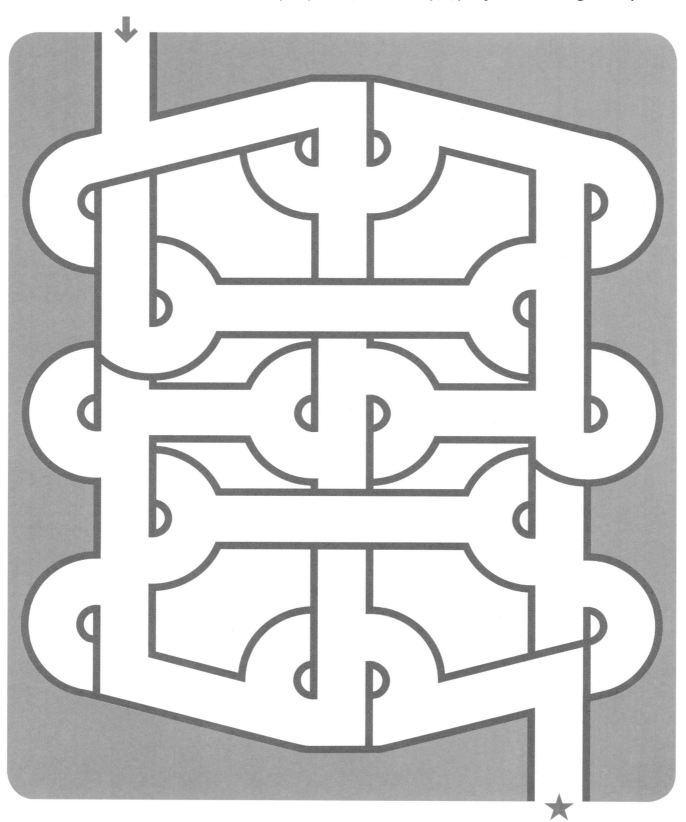

11 Dancing Pig

Name

Date

Draw a line from the arrow (→) to the star (★) by following the path.

Draw a line from the arrow (→) to the star (★) by following the path.

Tiger with a Torch

Draw a line from the arrow (→) to the star (★) by following the path.

Draw a line from the arrow (➡) to the star (★) by following the path.

Rabbit lifting a Barbell

Name

Date

Draw a line from the arrow (→) to the star (★) by following the path.

Draw a line from the arrow (→) to the star (★) by following the path.

 **Walking Chicken**

Name

Date

Draw a line from the arrow (→) to the star (★) by following the path.

Draw a line from the arrow (→) to the star (★) by following the path.

Jumping Mudskipper

Draw a line from the arrow (➡) to the star (★) by following the path.

Draw a line from the arrow (→) to the star (★) by following the path.

Skiing Wolf

Draw a line from the arrow (→) to the star (★) by following the path.

115

Draw a line from the arrow (→) to the star (★) by following the path.

17 Bear on a Skateboard

Name

Date

Draw a line from the arrow (→) to the star (★) by following the path.

117

Draw a line from the arrow (→) to the star (★) by following the path.

Name

Date

Draw a line from the arrow (→) to the star (★) by following the path.

Draw a line from the arrow (➡) to the star (★) by following the path.

19 First Place Elephant

Draw a line from the arrow (➡) to the star (★) by following the path.

121

Draw a line from the arrow (→) to the star (★) by following the path.

20 Raccoon Ninja

Name

Date

Draw a line from the arrow (➡) to the star (★) by following the path.

Draw a line from the arrow (→) to the star (★) by following the path.

Marshal Panda

Name

Date

Draw a line from the arrow (→) to the star (★) by following the path.

Draw a line from the arrow (→) to the star (★) by following the path.

Sergeant Bulldog

Name

Date

Draw a line from the arrow (➡) to the star (★) by following the path.

Draw a line from the arrow (→) to the star (★) by following the path.

23 Lion Firefighter

Draw a line from the arrow (➡) to the star (★) by following the path.

Draw a line from the arrow (→) to the star (★) by following the path.

24 Rock and Roll Bat

Name

Date

Draw a line from the arrow (➡) to the star (★) by following the path.

Draw a line from the arrow (→) to the star (★) by following the path.

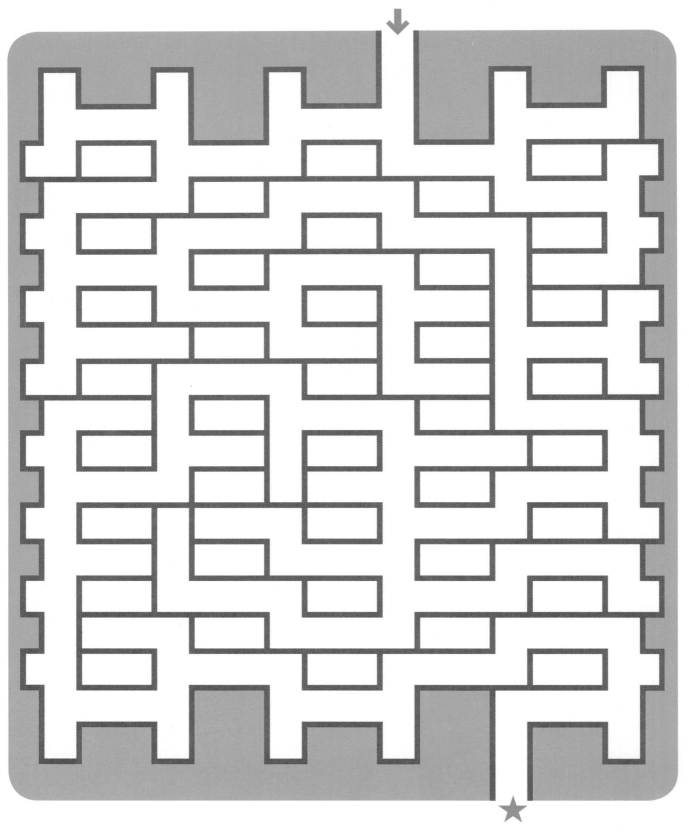

Name

Date

Draw a line from the arrow (→) to the star (★) by following the path.

Draw a line from the arrow (→) to the star (★) by following the path.

Hippo playing the Contrabass

Name

Date

Draw a line from the arrow (➡) to the star (★) by following the path.

Draw a line from the arrow (→) to the star (★) by following the path.

Bear playing the Cello

Name

Date

Draw a line from the arrow () to the star (★) by following the path.

Draw a line from the arrow (➡) to the star (★) by following the path.

28 | Dog playing the Saxophone

Name

Date

Draw a line from the arrow (→) to the star (★) by following the path.

139

Draw a line from the arrow (→) to the star (★) by following the path.

140

29 Pig playing the Sousaphone

Name

Date

Draw a line from the arrow (➡) to the star (★) by following the path.

Draw a line from the arrow (→) to the star (★) by following the path.

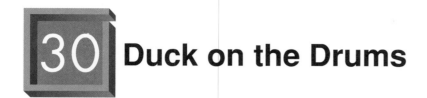

Name

Date

Draw a line from the arrow (→) to the star (★) by following the path.

Draw a line from the arrow (→) to the star (★) by following the path.

Growling Lion

Draw a line from the arrow (➡) to the star (★) by following the path.

Draw a line from the arrow (→) to the star (★) by following the path.

32 Elephant rowing a Boat

Name

Date

Draw a line from the arrow (➡) to the star (★) by following the path.

Draw a line from the arrow (→) to the star (★) by following the path.

33 Happy Sea Lion

Draw a line from the arrow (→) to the star (★) by following the path.

Draw a line from the arrow (➡) to the star (★) by following the path.

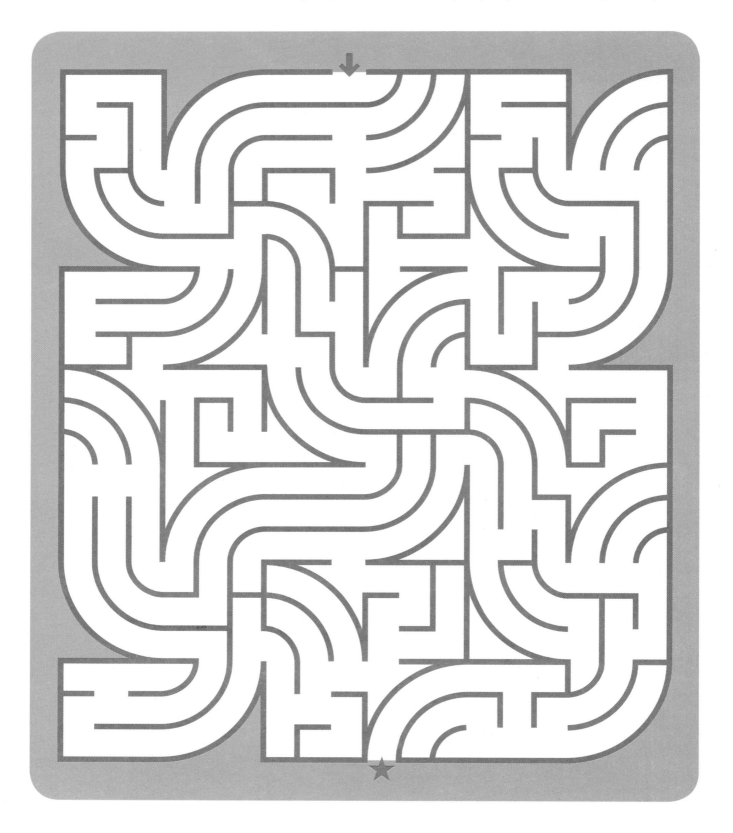

150

34 Two-Humped Camel

Draw a line from the arrow (➡) to the star (★) by following the path.

151

Draw a line from the arrow (→) to the star (★) by following the path.

Howling Wolf

Draw a line from the arrow () to the star (★) by following the path.

Draw a line from the arrow (→) to the star (★) by following the path.

36 **Balancing Hippo**

Draw a line from the arrow (➡) to the star (★) by following the path.

Draw a line from the arrow (→) to the star (★) by following the path.

Name

Date

Draw a line from the arrow (➡) to the star (★) by following the path.

Draw a line from the arrow (→) to the star (★) by following the path.

 **Triceratops**

Draw a line from the arrow (→) to the star (★) by following the path.

Draw a line from the arrow (→) to the star (⭐) by following the path.

Name

Date

Draw a line from the arrow (➡) to the star (★) by following the path.

Draw a line from the arrow (→) to the star (★) by following the path.

Stegosaurus

Name

Date

Draw a line from the arrow () to the star (★) by following the path.

Draw a line from the arrow (➡) to the star (★) by following the path.

164

My Big Book of MAZES

MAZES: AROUND THE WORLD

Table of Contents

In this section, your child will complete world landmark themed mazes to further hone his or her maze solving abilities. This section gives your child another opportunity to have fun and develop manual dexterity and pencil control. Children love to learn about new places, and they will enjoy the mazes in this section, which are full of geographical landmarks and famous buildings from around the world.

When your child has completed all the mazes in this section, you can use a map or a globe to help your child learn more about the world. On a map, children can see where the landmarks and buildings in the mazes they have completed are in relation to each other and learn more about the world.

The activities in this section will help your child develop pencil control and fine motor control, which are essential for early writing skills. If your child is interested in learning more about geography after completing this section, please refer to the appropriate book from our Sticker Activity Book series for further work.

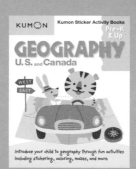 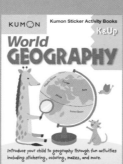  

GEOGRAPHY: U.S. and Canada Pre-K & Up

World GEOGRAPHY K & Up

SCIENCE Pre-K & Up

SCIENCE K & Up

How to hold a pencil properly

There are several ways to teach children to hold a pencil properly. Here is one example.

1 Help your child form an "L" shape with his or her thumb and forefinger as pictured here. Place the pencil against the top of the bent middle finger and on the thumb joint.

2 Now, have your child squeeze the pencil with the thumb and forefinger.

3 Check the way that your child is holding the pencil against the picture to decide whether or not it is the proper way.

It can be difficult for a child who does not yet have enough strength in his or her hand and fingers to hold the pencil properly. Please teach this skill gradually, so that your child will remaln interested and willing to hold a pencil naturally.

Statue of Liberty

Name

Date

To parents

Have your child trace a path through the maze with his or her finger before using a pencil. Next, have your child use a pencil to complete the maze. When your child is done, give him or her plenty of praise.

Draw a line from the arrow (➡) to the star (★) by following the path.

Draw a line from the arrow (→) to the star (★) by following the path.

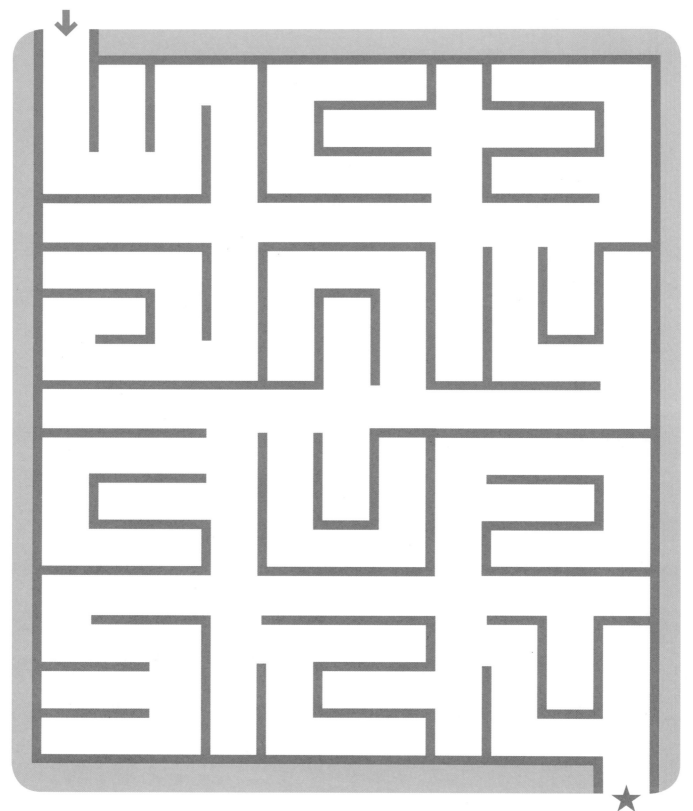

Stonehenge

United Kingdom

Name

Date

Draw a line from the arrow (➡) to the star (★) by following the path.

Draw a line from the arrow (➡) to the star (★) by following the path.

Chile

Moai Statues on Easter Island

Name

Date

To parents
Please help your child understand that the gray areas inside the maze are not obstacles. In other words, the correct path to the exit will take them through some of the gray shaded areas inside the maze.

Draw a line from the arrow (➡) to the star (★) by following the path.

171

Draw a line from the arrow (→) to the star (★) by following the path.

Mount Rushmore

United States of
America

Name

Date

Draw a line from the arrow (➡) to the star (★) by following the path.

Draw a line from the arrow (→) to the star (★) by following the path.

Cristo Redentor on Corcovado's Hill

Brazil

Draw a line from the arrow (→) to the star (★) by following the path.

175

Draw a line from the arrow (→) to the star (★) by following the path.

France

Mont-Saint-Michel

Draw a line from the arrow (→) to the star (★) by following the path.

177

Draw a line from the arrow (→) to the star (★) by following the path.

Japan

Great Buddha of Nara

Name

Date

Draw a line from the arrow (➡) to the star (★) by following the path.

Draw a line from the arrow (→) to the star (★) by following the path.

Australia

Ayers Rock

Name

Date

Draw a line from the arrow (→) to the star (★) by following the path.

Draw a line from the arrow (→) to the star (★) by following the path.

Tower Bridge

United Kingdom

Draw a line from the arrow (➡) to the star (★) by following the path.

183

Draw a line from the arrow (→) to the star (★) by following the path.

Mount Kilimanjaro

Name

Date

Draw a line from the arrow (➡) to the star (★) by following the path.

Draw a line from the arrow (→) to the star (★) by following the path.

Big Ben

United Kingdom

Draw a line from the arrow (→) to the star (★) by following the path.

187

Draw a line from the arrow (→) to the star (★) by following the path.

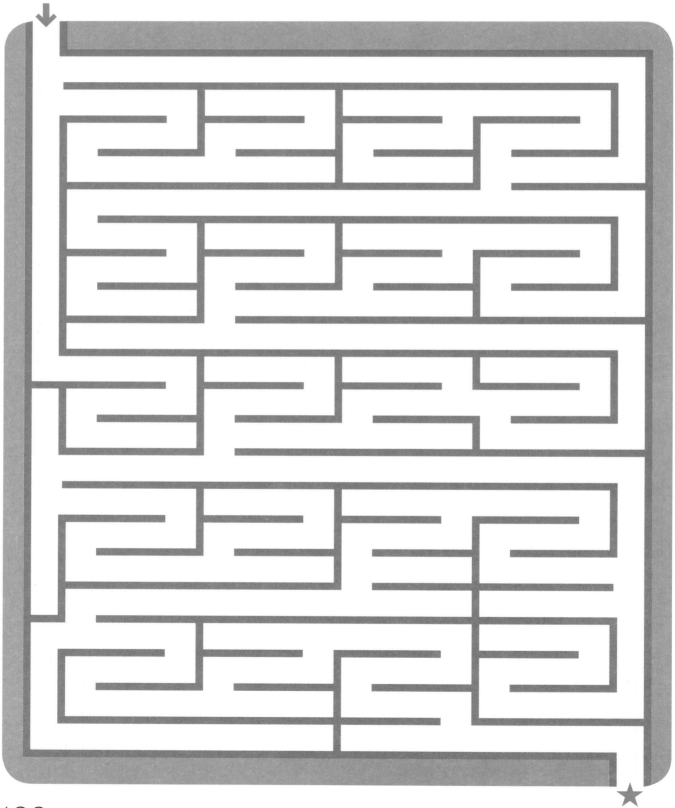

Michelangelo's Pieta

Name

Date

Draw a line from the arrow (→) to the star (★) by following the path.

189

Draw a line from the arrow (→) to the star (★) by following the path.

Draw a line from the arrow (➡) to the star (★) by following the path.

191

Draw a line from the arrow (→) to the star (★) by following the path.

Switzerland

Matterhorn

Draw a line from the arrow (➡) to the star (★) by following the path.

Draw a line from the arrow (→) to the star (★) by following the path.

194

Australia

Sydney Opera House

Draw a line from the arrow (➡) to the star (★) by following the path.

Draw a line from the arrow (→) to the star (★) by following the path.

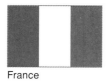

France

Arc de Triomphe

Draw a line from the arrow (➡) to the star (★) by following the path.

Draw a line from the arrow (→) to the star (★) by following the path.

Schloss Neuschwanstein

Germany

Draw a line from the arrow (➡) to the star (★) by following the path.

199

Draw a line from the arrow (→) to the star (★) by following the path.

200

Manhattan

United States of America

Name

Date

To parents

In mazes like this one, the colored parts of the illustration are obstacles. Please help your child understand that he or she cannot find an exit path through any illustration that is in color.

Draw a line from the arrow (➡) to the star (★) by following the path.

201

Draw a line from the arrow (→) to the star (★) by following the path.

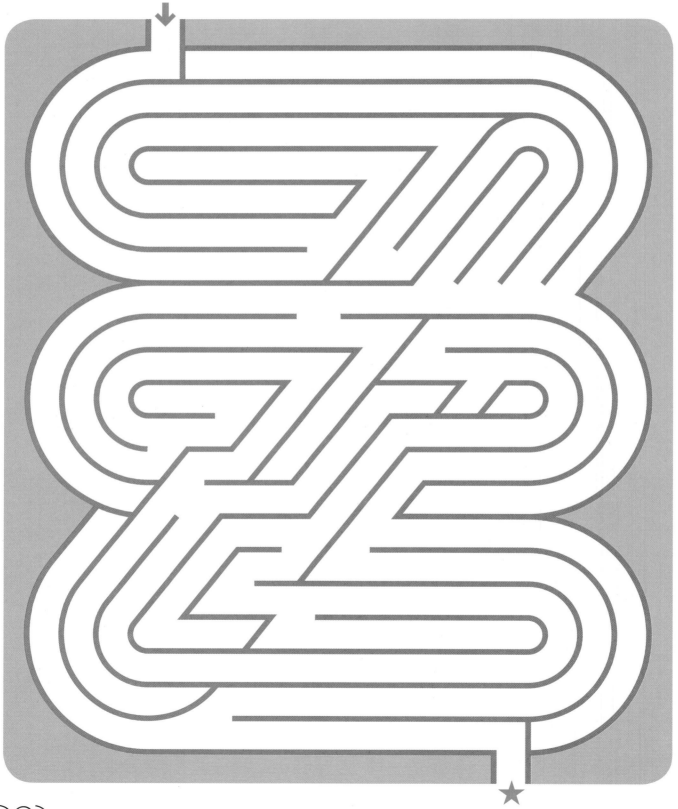

Pyramid at Chichen Itza

Name

Date

Draw a line from the arrow (➡) to the star (★) by following the path.

Draw a line from the arrow (→) to the star (★) by following the path.

Terracotta Warriors and Horses

China

Draw a line from the arrow (➡) to the star (★) by following the path.

Draw a line from the arrow (→) to the star (★) by following the path.

Golden Gate Bridge

Name

Date

Draw a line from the arrow (→) to the star (★) by following the path.

Draw a line from the arrow (→) to the star (★) by following the path.

Peru

Machu Picchu

Name

Date

Draw a line from the arrow (➡) to the star (★) by following the path.

209

Draw a line from the arrow (→) to the star (★) by following the path.

China

Forbidden City

Name

Date

Draw a line from the arrow (➡) to the star (★) by following the path.

Draw a line from the arrow (→) to the star (★) by following the path.

Niagara Falls

Canada

United States of America

Name

Date

Draw a line from the arrow (➡) to the star (★) by following the path.

Draw a line from the arrow (→) to the star (★) by following the path.

Parthenon

Greece

Name

Date

Draw a line from the arrow (➡) to the star (★) by following the path.

215

Draw a line from the arrow (→) to the star (★) by following the path.

Name

Date

Draw a line from the arrow (➡) to the star (★) by following the path.

Draw a line from the arrow (→) to the star (★) by following the path.

China

Great Wall of China

Name

Date

To parents

As your child progresses through this book, every maze is slightly harder than the last. If your child has a hard time, try giving him or her a hint.

Draw a line from the arrow (➡) to the star (★) by following the path.

Draw a line from the arrow (→) to the star (★) by following the path.

La Sagrada Familia

Draw a line from the arrow (➡) to the star (★) by following the path.

Draw a line from the arrow (→) to the star (★) by following the path.

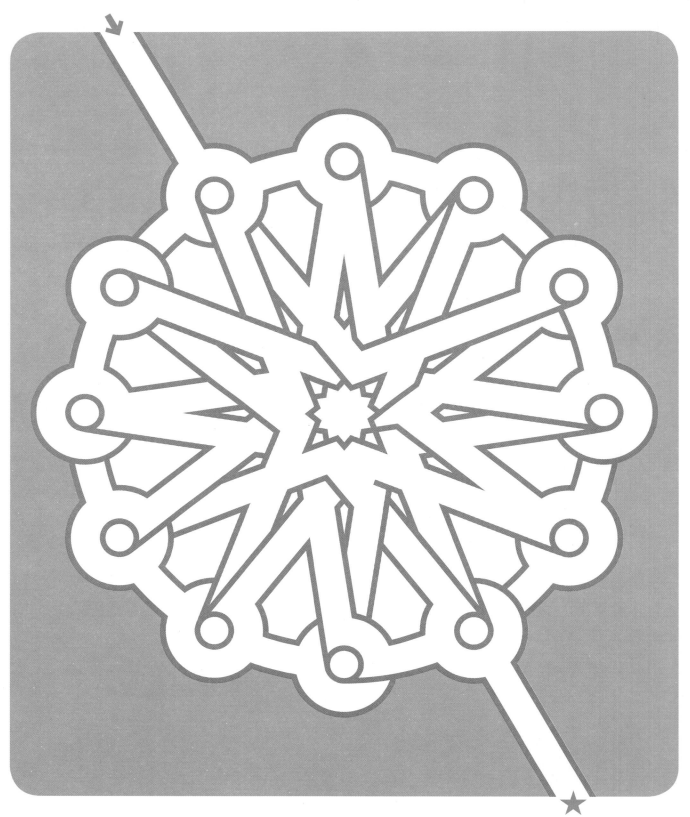

Basilica of the Sacre Coeur

Draw a line from the arrow (➡) to the star (★) by following the path.

223

Draw a line from the arrow (→) to the star (★) by following the path.

Cambodia

Angkor Thom

Draw a line from the arrow (→) to the star (★) by following the path.

225

Draw a line from the arrow (→) to the star (★) by following the path.

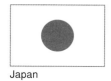

Japan

Himeji Castle

Name

Date

Draw a line from the arrow (➡) to the star (★) by following the path.

Draw a line from the arrow (→) to the star (★) by following the path.

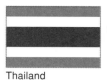
Thailand

Temple of the Dawn

Name

Date

Draw a line from the arrow (→) to the star (★) by following the path.

229

Draw a line from the arrow (→) to the star (★) by following the path.

Taj Mahal

India

Draw a line from the arrow (→) to the star (★) by following the path.

Draw a line from the arrow (→) to the star (★) by following the path.

Leaning Tower of Pisa

Italy

Draw a line from the arrow (➡) to the star (★) by following the path.

Draw a line from the arrow (➡) to the star (★) by following the path.

Mosque of
Muhammad Ali

Egypt

Draw a line from the arrow (→) to the star (★) by following the path.

235

Draw a line from the arrow (→) to the star (★) by following the path.

Italy

Ponte di Rialto

Draw a line from the arrow (→) to the star (★) by following the path.

237

Draw a line from the arrow (➡) to the star (★) by following the path.

Blue Mosque

Turkey

Name

Date

Draw a line from the arrow (➡) to the star (★) by following the path.

239

Draw a line from the arrow (→) to the star (★) by following the path.

Italy

The Duomo of Florence

Draw a line from the arrow (➡) to the star (★) by following the path.

241

Draw a line from the arrow (➡) to the star (★) by following the path.

Japan

East Tower in
Yakushi-ji Temple

Name

Date

Draw a line from the arrow (→) to the star (★) by following the path.

Draw a line from the arrow (→) to the star (★) by following the path.

244

Russia

Saint Basil's
Cathedral in Red Square

Name

Date

Draw a line from the arrow (➡) to the star (★) by following the path.

To parents

Did your child enjoy these mazes? When your child is finished, compare this page with the first few pages of this section. You will see considerable progress in his or her ability to control a pencil. Please give praise for your child's effort and achievement.

Draw a line from the arrow (➡) to the star (★) by following the path.

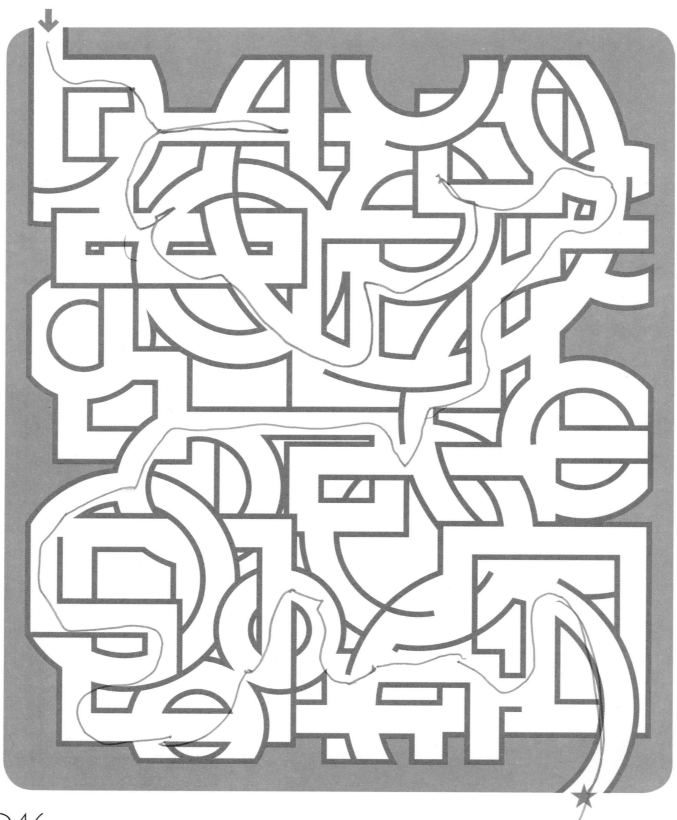

KUMON

Certificate of **Achievement**

....

is hereby congratulated on completing

My Big Book of MAZES

Presented on .... , 20

....

Parent or Guardian